Dedication

For Cam

You were my deepest heartbreak and my greatest teacher.

Through the light, the dark, and everything in between.

This book carries forward the strength, the love, your life and your death awakened in me.

Always

Kerri

Strength Through Struggle

An Introduction to The CAMS Method to Overcome Challenges and Thrive Through Life's Trials

By Kerri Humble

Contents

Introduction

If you're holding this book, you're probably going through something. Or maybe you've come through it, but your heart still carries echoes of it. Loss. Change. Grief. Growth. Burnout. Breakups. Life.

This book isn't here to fix you, because you're not broken. It's here to walk beside you. To hold space for you. To remind you that you're not alone, and you're not doing it wrong.

Inside, you'll find stories, tools, mindset shifts, and raw reflections from my own journey—through grief, healing, rebuilding, and the wild process of becoming.

The CAMS Method was born from personal

experience, not theory. It stands for Clarity, Acceptance, Movement, and Support—four pillars that helped me not just survive, but grow stronger, wiser, and more *me*.

My hope is that it does the same for you.

You don't have to be perfect. You just have to be willing. Willing to feel, to reflect, to play, to shift, to heal, to rise.

Let's begin.

Chapter 1

Finding Light in the Dark

Chapter 1: Finding Light in the Dark

There are moments in life that drop you to your knees. Moments when everything you thought was stable gets stripped away — and you're left blinking in the dark, wondering how you'll ever find your way through.

For me, one of those moments came in June 2020, in the early days of the coronavirus pandemic. My husband Cam — my person, my challenger, my mirror — died unexpectedly after an accident at home. He had to have brain surgery and was recovering well in hospital, but due to COVID restrictions, I wasn't allowed to visit him.

One morning, a few days after his surgery, I got a call saying things had "taken a turn" and I should make my way to the hospital. I didn't understand at the time — I was naïve. I didn't realise that call was actually a warning that he couldn't be resuscitated.

When he passed, the grief was heavy — and compounded by the isolation the pandemic forced upon us. We weren't allowed to hug our loved ones. We weren't allowed to gather in groups. His funeral was limited to 20 people, all seated apart, all aching in silence. I had to drive behind the hearse for 45 minutes to his crematorium service — my children in the car with me, all of us trying to stay strong while holding an unbearable grief. No one to hug. No shared comfort. Just our little unit in the car, holding each other together the best we could.

And still… I got through it.

The CAMS Method was born from that time. From the mess, the heartbreak, the rage, the numbness, and the raw need to survive something unthinkable. It came from my lived experience — not as a guru or a therapist, but as someone who had to claw her way back to life.

This chapter of your life — whatever it looks like — may feel unbearable too. But I want you to know: there is light ahead. Maybe not the light you had before. Maybe not what you expected. But something softer, wiser, and more honest waits on the other side.

And until you reach it, this book will walk with you.

Because you're not broken. You're becoming.

Chapter 2

The Ripple Effect

Chapter 2: The Ripple Effect

Healing isn't selfish.

In fact, healing yourself is one of the most generous things you can do for the world.

When you shift, it touches everyone around you. Your energy changes. Your voice softens. Your strength returns. Your courage becomes contagious.

That's the ripple effect.

It starts with you deciding to take care of yourself. To choose clarity over confusion. To choose peace over chaos. To choose presence, even when it's painful.

When you do that, others notice. They begin to feel permission to do the same.

You don't need a huge platform to make an impact. You don't need a perfect life. You don't even need to have all the answers.

You just need to begin.

Healing Creates Waves

Think about how one kind word from a stranger can change your day. How one conversation can shift your mindset. How one person's courage can inspire a whole community.

That's what you're doing every time you choose to

heal.

You're creating ripples that go beyond what you'll ever see.

You might never know the full impact of your healing.

But someone else will feel it. And they might pass it on.

Let your journey be a ripple.

Let your growth reach places you never imagined.

Let this be the start of something far bigger than just you.

Chapter 3

The CAMS Method

A Framework for Growth

Chapter 3: The CAMS Method — A Framework for Growth

Comfort. Acceptance. Mindset. Self.

CAMS Method was born not out of theory, but out of lived experience — from deep grief, raw survival, and the determination to find a way through when life broke apart.

It's named after Cam, not because he lived by these steps, but because his life, love, and loss taught me lessons that shaped this method. In a way, this work keeps his name — and the ripples of who he was — alive.

There's a saying:

> *"You die twice — once when you take your last breath, and again when your name is spoken for the last time."*
> CAMS Method is my way of keeping his name, and the lessons I learned through loving and losing him, alive.

It's also a method for *you* — a guide to find footing when the ground falls away.

CAMS isn't just about surviving grief. It's designed to help with any deep struggle: loss, trauma, change, identity shifts.

It's **simple, powerful, and deeply personal** — and it's flexible enough to meet you wherever you are.

This is just an introduction. In time, CAMS will be taught more deeply — through workbooks, courses, and practitioner training — but for now, I want you to meet the heart of it.

C — Comfort

When you are shattered, you don't need motivation posters.

You don't need someone to tell you to "stay positive."

You need *comfort* — small, real, reachable things that make breathing possible again.

Comfort is the first pillar because **relief comes before rebuilding**.

Comfort can be:

- Wrapping yourself in a hoodie that smells like home

- Putting on music that lifts you even 2%

- Crying in the shower without judging yourself

- Cuddling a dog, a blanket, a memory

It's about **offering yourself tenderness** — without needing to be "fixed" first.
 It's about recognising that you are hurting, and meeting yourself with softness instead of shame.

A — Acceptance

Acceptance is not approval.

It's not giving up.

It's simply **stopping the war** against what has already happened.

For me, acceptance meant whispering:

> *"This is my reality now. I didn't choose it. I don't have to like it. But it's real."*

Acceptance allows healing energy to move. Without it, we stay stuck in resistance, burning out from trying to fight reality.

Acceptance looks like:

- Naming the truth, even if it's ugly

- Letting yourself grieve the unfairness without pretending

- Saying *yes* to this moment, *even when it hurts like hell*

It doesn't mean you have to like the loss.
It means you stop denying it, so you can finally begin to live *with* it, not against it.

M — Mindset

Mindset work saved me.

But not in the polished, Instagram-affirmations way.
Real mindset work, in my darkest times, looked like choosing thoughts that **eased** my suffering — even slightly.

When my mind said, "I can't do this,"
I practiced replacing it with, "I am doing it, even though it feels impossible."

When I spiraled, I asked:

> *"Is this thought helping me or hurting me right now?"*

Mindset is not about *perfect positivity*.
It's about **tipping your thoughts slightly toward relief**, again and again, until you find a tiny foothold in the dark.

Mindset shifts are powerful because they compound. One better-feeling thought can lead to one better-feeling action, which leads to momentum, which leads to hope.

S — Self

After devastation, rebuilding always leads back to **Self**.

You aren't who you were before.
You can't be.
Loss changes you — deeply, permanently.

But it doesn't destroy you.

Self is the place you come home to.
It's where you reconnect with your worth, your instincts, your creativity, your desires.

Self-work inside CAMS means:

- Rebuilding self-compassion (how you talk to yourself)

- Rebuilding self-trust (listening to your gut)

- Rebuilding self-expression (letting yourself create, speak, dance, move, feel)

This isn't about becoming your "old self."
It's about **becoming the self who survived — and grew anyway.**

Closing Thoughts on CAMS

You don't have to "master" all of CAMS to benefit.
 You don't have to do it perfectly.
 You can start anywhere. Some days will be pure Comfort.
 Some days will be tiny shifts in mindset.
 Some days will simply be breathing.

CAMS is a method built with tenderness, not pressure.
 It's a hand you can hold when you feel alone.

This is just the beginning.
 Later, there will be deeper guides, practitioner training, expanded workbooks, and live teaching.
 But for now — this is your helpful hand to grab onto.

CAMS

Comfort. Acceptance. Mindset. Self.

 A lifeline when you need it most.

Chapter 4

SELF

Rebuilding the Relationship with You

Chapter 4: SELF — Rebuilding the Relationship with You

The SELF section of the CAMS Method is where we turn inward and start rewriting the story we tell ourselves. It's where healing deepens, confidence rebuilds, and your inner voice goes from critic to cheerleader.

SELF isn't one thing — it's a layered, evolving connection with yourself that includes self-love, self-worth, self-trust, and more. This chapter breaks it down so you can reconnect with who you really are underneath the pain, the pressure, and the performance.

Self-Love

This is the foundation. Self-love isn't bubble baths and candles (though those are lovely). It's about how you speak to yourself, how you show up for yourself, and how you honour your needs.

Try This

Write a letter to yourself from the most loving, compassionate version of you. Read it when your inner critic gets loud.

Self-Worth

Your worth is not tied to your productivity, your appearance, or your past. It is *inherent*. This part of the journey is about unlearning the lie that you have to earn your value.

Try This

Make a list of things that make you valuable that have nothing to do with what you do for others.

Self-Awareness

You can't change what you're not aware of. This is about noticing your triggers, your patterns, and your beliefs without judgment. Awareness is power.

Try This

For one day, keep a note of moments you felt reactive. Later, ask: What was really going on underneath?

Self-Reflection

This is the part where you pause and take stock. What's working? What's not? What am I learning about myself? Reflection helps you recalibrate with clarity.

Try This

Weekly check-ins with yourself. Ask: What did I do well? What do I want to shift?

Self-Compassion

Speak to yourself like someone you love. Especially when you feel like a mess. This isn't about letting yourself off the hook—it's about understanding that you're human.

Try This

When you mess up, say: "Of course I felt that way. Of course I did that. I'm still worthy."

Self-Expression

Let yourself be seen. Whether it's through art, fashion, voice, writing, or dancing — your truth is meant to be expressed. This part of the journey helps you stop shrinking.

Try This

Ask yourself: What am I not saying that needs to be said? What part of me is craving more freedom?

Self-Empowerment

This is about choice. Boundaries. Speaking up. Moving from victim energy into personal power. Self-empowerment says: *I get to choose how I respond.*

Try This

Make a list of things that drain your energy, and choose one to release or say no to this week.

Self-Respect

Respect means honouring your time, energy, and values. It means walking away from what dims your light and standing firm in your truth.

Try This

Write a list of your non-negotiables in relationships, work, and daily life.

Self-Trust

This is deep. It's built by keeping promises to yourself
and listening to your own inner guidance. It grows
every time you choose what feels right for *you*.

Try This

*Reflect on a time you listened to your gut and it
worked out. Let that be proof you can trust yourself.*

Self-Sabotage

We all do it. This is where you look at the ways you've
protected yourself by staying small, avoiding change,

or numbing out. Not to shame yourself, but to understand.

Try This

Ask: If I really believed I was worthy of everything I want… what would I stop doing?

Final Note on SELF

The relationship you have with yourself is the longest one you'll ever have. It deserves your care. Your softness. Your truth. You are not broken — you are becoming.

The more you meet yourself with compassion and courage, the more life starts to shift around you. SELF isn't a destination. It's a practice. One that changes everything.

Chapter 5

Comfort & Grounding

Tools for When It's Hard

Chapter 5: Comfort & Grounding — Tools for When It's Hard

When life shakes you, you need something to hold onto. Something that reminds you: *you are safe, you are here, and you can breathe through this.*

This chapter is about those tools. The ones you reach for when your thoughts spiral, when grief hits like a wave, when your nervous system is fried or your emotions feel too big. These are the things that soothe your system and help you anchor back into yourself.

You don't need to fix everything. Sometimes, you just need to feel *held*. These practices help you do exactly that.

1. Sensory Comfort

Your senses are powerful portals to the present moment. When you engage them intentionally, they can calm your nervous system and create instant relief.

Try This

- Wrap yourself in something soft and warm

- Light a familiar, comforting scent (a candle, oil, or even your partner's jumper)

- Sip something warm and nourishing

- Press your hand to your heart and notice the rhythm

Let your body know: *I'm safe now.*

2. Comforting Self-Talk

We all need someone to say, "You're okay. I've got you." Sometimes, that someone has to be *you*.

Try This

Write down words that soothe you. Things like:

- "It's okay to feel like this."

- "You're doing the best you can."

- "I'm proud of you for showing up."

Read them out loud when you're wobbly. Record them in your own voice. Let your inner cheerleader speak louder than your inner critic.

---

3. Imagining Connection

When someone we love is gone or far away, we can still feel their presence. You can call on that energy when you need comfort.

Try This

- Close your eyes and imagine them sitting beside you

- Hear their voice telling you what you most need to hear

- Feel their love wrapping around you

You can even write yourself a message from them. What would they say to you right now? Let that love flow through.

---

4. Breathing to Ground

The breath is always with you. It's a built-in grounding tool, and it costs nothing.

Try This

- Inhale for 4, hold for 4, exhale for 6

- Place your feet flat on the floor and feel the ground beneath you

- Name 5 things you can see, 4 you can touch, 3 you can hear, 2 you can smell, and 1 you can taste

This brings you back into the *now*. *And the now is always survivable.*

---

5. Movement for Release

Sometimes your body holds emotion that your mind can't process. Movement helps it move through.

Try This

- Put on one song and dance it out — no choreography, just feeling

- Shake your hands, arms, and legs for 30 seconds

- Stretch your body slowly, with intention

This isn't about fitness. It's about freedom.

---

6. Grounding Objects or Rituals

Having something physical to hold or focus on can keep you anchored.

Try This

- Carry a crystal, stone, or talisman that feels meaningful

- Use a weighted blanket or eye mask

- Create a mini comfort kit with items that soothe you

- Make tea slowly and mindfully as a ritual

Let these little things remind you: *you have tools, and you are not alone.*

---

7. Recognising Triggers and Creating Safety

Sometimes a smell, sound, or phrase can suddenly throw you off. Knowing your triggers helps you respond with care.

Try This

- Write down known triggers and how they affect you

- Make a list of ways to soothe yourself when they happen

- Let people close to you know how to support you

You deserve to feel safe in your body and in your space.

Final Thoughts on Comfort & Grounding

There is no weakness in needing comfort. There is no shame in needing softness. You are not meant to be strong all the time.

These tools are your anchors. Your reset buttons. Your reminders that even when things feel messy or overwhelming, you can return to yourself.

You are never too far gone. You are always worthy of gentleness. And you get to find peace in the small things.

Let comfort be sacred. Let grounding be your home.

Chapter 6

Reframing Loss — From What's Missing to What's Gained

Chapter 6: Reframing Loss — From What's Missing to What's Gained

Loss cracks us open. It can feel like a tearing, a hollowing out. Whether it's the death of a loved one, the end of a relationship, a life you thought you'd have, or a version of yourself you've outgrown — loss leaves space.

And in that space, you get to decide what grows.

This chapter isn't about silver linings or toxic positivity. It's about choosing to honour what was *while also* noticing what's been gained. The love. The lessons. The strength. The softness. The expansion.

Because yes, something is gone. But something else has emerged.

A Shift in Perspective

When we focus only on what we've lost, we sit in a space of lack. It feels heavy. Closed. Isolating. But when we begin to gently shift our perspective and ask, *"What have I gained from knowing this person? From living this experience?"* — something softens.

That doesn't erase the pain. It *reframes* it.

You can miss someone and still smile at the memories. You can grieve a chapter of your life and still appreciate the strength it gave you.

Try This

Write down 3 things you have gained because of what you lost. A lesson. A way you grew. A deeper connection to someone or something.

Loss as Expansion

Loss can stretch your heart in ways nothing else can. It makes you more empathetic. More tender. More attuned to what really matters.

In the empty space, you learn to listen. To slow down. To show up differently.

You gain new lenses. New compassion. New depth.

You might even find a sense of purpose you never expected. A calling. A message. A mission to carry forward. Like a ripple.

Grief Doesn't Mean Disconnection

One of the hardest parts of loss is the feeling that someone is just... gone.

But energy doesn't disappear. It transforms. And so does connection.

You can still talk to them. Feel them. Laugh with them in your mind. *Carry their love forward in how you live.*

Try This

Have a conversation with them. In writing. In your head. Out loud. Tell them what you wish they knew. Listen for what they'd say back.

This isn't imagination. This is soul memory.

Rituals to Honour What Was

Sometimes we need to mark the loss. Create a moment. Honour the impact.

Ideas

- Light a candle and speak their name

- Make a playlist of songs that remind you of them

- Plant something and let it grow in their memory

- Write their best qualities on pieces of paper and keep them in a jar

Let the love live on *through* you.

Letting Loss Shape You, Not Define You

You are not only what you've lost.

You are what you've lived through.

What you've felt deeply.

What you've held and released.

Let this chapter of your life be *part* of your story, not the whole thing.

Let it shape you with wisdom and heart, not close you off in fear.

You're still here. Still becoming.

And that in itself is something you've gained.

Chapter 7

Conversations with the Unseen — Staying Connected

Chapter 7: Conversations with the Unseen — Staying Connected

Just because someone is no longer physically here doesn't mean the connection is gone. Energy continues. Love continues. And in quiet moments, if you allow it, you can still feel them.

This chapter is about those conversations. The ones we have with loved ones who have passed. With future versions of ourselves. With the Universe. With the unseen support that holds us, even when we feel alone.

You don't have to be spiritual to feel this. You just have to be open.

Still Talking, Still Listening

After loss, it can feel strange to keep talking to someone who's no longer here. But it's not strange at all. It's sacred.

Your love didn't end. Why should your conversations?

Try This

- Speak to them out loud when you're driving, walking, or before bed

- Write them letters

- Ask a question and wait for a feeling, a memory, a lyric, or a sign

Sometimes the answers don't come in words — they come in chills, songs, sudden peace, or belly buzzes. *Trust what you feel.*

Signs, Symbols & Synchronicity

The universe speaks in symbols. That fox you keep seeing. That feather. That number that keeps repeating. That song on the radio right when you needed it.

These aren't coincidences. They're moments of connection.

Ask for a sign

Be playful about it. "Cam, if you're around today, send me something pink." And then go about your day. Don't look for it. Let it come.

This isn't proof. It's presence.

Future You Has Wisdom Too

You can also connect with the version of you who already made it through this. The one who's a little older, wiser, freer.

Try This

- Sit in stillness and imagine Future You standing beside you

- *Ask*: What would they say? How would they guide you through this?

- Let your voice be calm, kind, and clear

Future You is not separate. It's you, just a little further ahead.

The Universe Has Your Back

If you believe in something bigger — God, Source, the Universe, energy, Love with a capital L — you can lean on it.

Talk to it like it's a friend. A mentor. A quiet, steady presence always within reach.

Try This

- Before you start your day, say: "Show me what I need to know."

- When things feel tough, whisper: "Help me see this differently."

- At night, thank life for one thing that felt kind

It doesn't matter what name you use. What matters is that you feel supported.

You Are Never Alone

The unseen doesn't mean imaginary. It means *intuitive*. Felt. Known. Remembered.

Whether it's your loved one, your soul, your guides, your future self, or the vast love that holds this whole universe together — you are never walking this road alone.

So speak. Listen. Trust.

The conversation is still happening.

And the connection is still real.

Chapter 8

Energy and Continuity

Chapter 8: Energy and Continuity

One of the most comforting ideas I've ever come across is this: energy cannot be created or destroyed — it can only be transformed.

This truth, rooted in physics, also speaks to something deeper. The essence of who we are — our love, our presence, our spirit — doesn't just disappear. It shifts. It evolves. It continues.

This chapter isn't here to tell you what to believe. It's here to offer a perspective that has soothed me through grief, helped me find peace with loss, and reminded me that connection never truly ends.

Everything Is Energy

Your thoughts. Your feelings. Your body. The wind. The ocean. Music. Memories. Connection. It's all energy.

When someone dies, their physical form is gone — but the energy of who they were, what they brought to your life, how they made you feel — that still lingers.

It transforms.

Love Doesn't Vanish

You've felt this. When you hear their laugh in your head. When you instinctively go to message them. When you dream about them or suddenly feel surrounded by their presence.

That's not fantasy. That's continuity.

Love is energy. And energy continues.

Rituals of Remembering

Keeping a connection alive doesn't mean living in the past. It means acknowledging that what you shared is part of you now. You carry them forward — in how you love, how you live, how you show up.

Try This

- Create a ritual of remembrance — lighting a candle, playing their song, walking their favourite route

- Speak to them when you need to — and pause to listen, too

- Write down signs you've noticed — even the small ones

Energy as Legacy

Think about the ripple effect of one kind person. How their energy influences a whole room. How their words, their comfort, or their presence impacted you.

You are someone's ripple too.

Whether they're still here or not, the energy exchanged between you lives on — in your choices, your growth, your legacy.

You Are Energy Too

This chapter isn't just about those we've lost. It's also about *you*.

You are energy in motion. Constantly shifting. Becoming. Radiating. That's why your healing matters. Your joy matters. Your thoughts matter.

What you do with your energy becomes your ripple.

So choose love. Choose intention. Choose to believe, even just a little, that nothing meaningful is ever really lost.

Only transformed.

Chapter 9

Manifestation, Mindset & Mischief

Chapter 9: Manifestation, Mindset & Mischief

Let's talk about manifestation — but in a way that's grounded, cheeky, and totally resistance-free.

Manifestation isn't just about vision boards and scripting. It's about energy, belief, intention, and fun. It's about tuning your frequency to what you *want* instead of what you fear. And most importantly? *It's about feeling good now* — even before the thing arrives.

Because when you feel good, you attract more things that feel good. That's not magic. That's alignment.

Mindset Comes First

The stories you tell yourself shape your reality. Every thought is a mini manifestation in progress. When you change your inner narrative, your outer world starts to shift too.

Try This

Notice your dominant thoughts. Are they rooted in lack or in possibility? Are you expecting disappointment, or leaving room for miracles?

Shift gently. Start with, *"What if this works out better than I imagined?"*

The "Wouldn't It Be Nice..." Game

This one's straight from Esther Hicks and it's a game-changer. It's the manifestation tool that sidesteps resistance and invites curiosity.

Play It Like This

- Wouldn't it be nice if I felt really clear today?

- Wouldn't it be nice if I got an unexpected order?

- Wouldn't it be nice if something magical happened this week?

This softens your energy. It opens you up. It makes manifestation feel playful instead of pressured.

Resistance-Free Requests

Sometimes, we want to believe — but doubt creeps in. That's when you shift from manifesting something *big* to manifesting something *neutral*.

Try This

- Ask to see someone in red shoes

- Ask for a feather or a heart-shaped stone

- Ask to overhear someone say a funny phrase

When it shows up — even in a TV show or a book — it's proof: *you are co-creating with something bigger than you.* This builds belief.

Mischief as Medicine

Serious energy can be sticky. When you're gripping too hard to an outcome, you clog up the flow.

So get silly. Dance. Daydream. Flirt with the universe. Wear glitter. Make up a character who lives your dream life and pretend you're her for the day.

The Universe loves mischief. And so does your nervous system.

Align Before You Hustle

Action is important. But energy comes first. Don't just do things to make things happen — feel into what already wants to happen through you.

Try This

Before working on a goal, pause and ask, *"How do I want to feel while doing this?"* Then choose actions that match that frequency.

When your energy leads, the actions land better. They ripple wider. They feel lighter.

Final Thoughts on Manifesting

You don't have to be perfect to manifest beautiful things. You don't need to control the timing. You don't need to be endlessly high-vibe.

You just need to soften into belief.

Manifestation is simply this: tuning into the life you want, and gently becoming a match for it.

Let it be light.

Let it be cheeky.

Let it be yours.

Chapter 10

Strength Through Struggle

The Marathon Story

Chapter 10: Strength Through Struggle — The Marathon Story

I never set out to run a marathon. It was a spontaneous idea, the kind you almost laugh at for even considering. I hadn't done any running or sports since school. I was 36 years old when I ran the Edinburgh Marathon in 2017 — with just six weeks of training. Well, more like five, if I'm honest.

But I signed up. And I did it.

The story of that marathon has become a metaphor I return to over and over again. Not because I ran fast, or won medals, or crossed the finish line with ease — but because I kept going. Through the doubt. Through the pain. Through the moments I wanted to give up. And I didn't walk a single step of it.

Running With Cam

At the time, my husband Cam was alive and ran the marathon with me. He struggled throughout. He complained. He stopped often. He gave me a hard time, and to be honest, that reflected how he could be with me in life, too. There were moments his energy was heavy, even aggressive. But I needed to keep going.

So I ran ahead. I ran on the spot when he stopped. I stayed in motion, even when everything in me wanted to rest.

The goal I set for myself was this: *Don't walk. Keep running. No matter what.*

It became symbolic. I wasn't just running the marathon. I was running through life's hardest moments. I was proving to myself that I could keep going even when the path wasn't smooth, even when the person beside me wasn't holding me up.

The Power of Grit

There were moments that tested me — mentally, physically, emotionally. But I kept going. Not because I wasn't tired. Not because it was easy. But because I knew, deep down, that I was capable of more than I'd ever believed.

Crossing that finish line was one of the most emotional moments of my life. Not just because I did it — but because I did it for *me*. I didn't stop. I didn't let someone else's struggle become my excuse. I didn't fall into old patterns of shrinking myself.

And the wildest part? I could've kept running. A part of me *wanted* to keep going. Because I had more in me.

Why This Story Matters

This story isn't about running. It's about resilience. It's about grit. It's about that fire inside you that says, *"No. I won't stop here."*

We all have a marathon moment in our lives. Maybe yours isn't 26.2 miles. Maybe it's grief. Or divorce. Or rebuilding after being broken. Maybe it's getting up each day when you don't feel strong enough. Maybe it's carrying others while trying to hold yourself up.

Whatever it is, this chapter is your reminder:

You are stronger than you think.

You have more in the tank.

You are allowed to lead yourself forward, even if no one else can.

Your struggle is not your stopping point. It's your strength story in motion.

Chapter 11

The Only Constant is Change

Chapter 11: The Only Constant is Change

Change is the one thing we can count on. Seasons change. People change. We change. And while change can feel terrifying, it can also be liberating.

This chapter is a gentle invitation to make peace with change — to stop resisting it and start flowing with it. Because the truth is, when we learn to honour change, we open ourselves up to transformation.

Nature is Our Reminder

Look at the seasons. Spring never clings to winter. Leaves fall without fighting it. The tides move in and out with trust. Nature doesn't resist change — it embodies it.

And so do we.

We're meant to grow. To evolve. To release. To begin again. And again. And again.

Try This

Think about a past version of you. Who were you 5 years ago? What have you outgrown? What are you proud of becoming?

Grieving the Old While Welcoming the New

Change often comes with grief. Even good change can bring sadness. You can be excited for what's ahead *and* mourn what's behind you.

This is especially true when you're letting go of relationships, identities, or beliefs that once defined you.

You don't have to pretend it's easy. But you do get to trust that change is leading you somewhere new.

Try This

Write a goodbye letter to the version of you or the season you're leaving behind. Thank it. Let it go with grace.

Perspective Shifts Everything

When change feels scary, ask yourself:

- What is this making space for?

- What am I learning about myself?

- What could this turn into if I allowed it?

Most of the time, fear of change is fear of the unknown. But the unknown is also where *all* new possibilities live.

You Are Allowed to Change, Too

You are not who you were last year.

You are not who you were before the loss.

You are not defined by your past.

You are allowed to change your mind.

To change your path.

To change your energy, your truth, your boundaries, your dreams.

Changing doesn't mean you were wrong. It means you're *becoming*.

Final Thoughts on Change

Change will find you, whether you're ready or not. But how you move through it is where your power lies.

You can brace against it, or you can breathe through it.

You can fear it, or you can get curious.

You can grieve it, and you can grow from it.

Either way, you are not stuck. You are not broken.

You are becoming. And change is your proof.

Chapter 12

Your Next Chapter

Becoming the Ripple

Chapter 12: Your Next Chapter — Becoming the Ripple

If you've made it this far, you already are the ripple. Whether you know it or not, your healing, your growth, your courage to keep going — it echoes. It touches others. It inspires quietly and powerfully.

You don't need to have it all figured out. You don't need to be fully healed or wildly successful or endlessly high-vibe. You just need to keep choosing to show up for yourself with honesty, compassion, and intention.

That's how the ripple begins.

From Surviving to Leading

You've survived things that changed you. You've met yourself in your hardest moments. You've rebuilt from rubble and found your way forward through grief, growth, change, and self-discovery.

Now it's time to lead — not with ego, but with heart. Lead by living your truth. Lead by giving others permission to do the same. Lead by example, not perfection.

What You Share, Heals Others

Every time you tell your story, someone breathes easier. Every time you speak your truth, someone feels less alone. Every time you heal, you change the energy in the room.

This is the ripple effect.

You might never know how far it travels. But trust me — it does.

The Legacy of Your Becoming

You came through things you didn't think you'd survive. You found strength you didn't know you had. You chose softness in a hard world.

That is a legacy.

Whether you leave behind a book, a method, a conversation, a moment of kindness, or just a different way of being — you are leaving a mark. A beautiful, bold, gentle mark on the people around you.

You Are the Beginning

Not the end.

Not the pause.

Not the aftermath.

You are the beginning of something new.

A new way of loving.

A new way of showing up.

A new way of healing.

Keep choosing yourself.

Keep leading with truth.

Keep rippling outward.

Because your next chapter?

It starts right now.

Outro

A Love Note for the Road Ahead

Outro: A Love Note for the Road Ahead

Thank you for walking this journey with me. For opening this book, for opening your heart, for choosing to move forward when staying stuck might have felt easier.

I hope this book reminded you of your strength, your softness, your resilience, and your magic. I hope it gave you comfort. Tools. A sense of being seen. And maybe even a spark.

You don't need to remember everything you read here. Just hold onto what resonated. Let the rest come back to you when you need it most.

You are allowed to be a masterpiece and a work-in-progress all at once.

Keep choosing yourself.

Keep rising.

Keep rippling.

I'm so proud of you.

About the Author

Kerri Humble is a life coach, creative, and resilience mentor who knows what it means to break — and rebuild.

After becoming widowed at 39, following the sudden death of her husband Cam during the early days of the coronavirus pandemic, Kerri was thrown into a deep grief made heavier by isolation. Unable to visit him in hospital, say goodbye properly, or hug loved ones at the funeral, she experienced loss in one of the most disconnected times in modern history.

From that space, she created the CAMS Method — a practical, soulful approach to navigating grief, overwhelm, and identity shifts. It became her anchor, her guide, and her way back to herself.

Kerri now blends heart, humour, and healing to help others rise through their own struggles. Through her book, coaching, and creative work, she invites others to see that they're not broken — they're becoming.

She lives in Northumberland, UK, and is the founder of LOOP Emporium, Berwick Upon Tweed — a bold, soul-led gift shop with a rebellious streak and a high-vibe heart.

https://linktr.ee/kerri.humble

Reflections & Notes

Printed in Great Britain
by Amazon

62880681R00067